Only the Ravens Care

A Collection of Poems by

William A. Roberts

A.H. STOCKWELL
PUBLISHERS SINCE 1898

Published in 2024 by
William A. Roberts
East Malling, Kent
in association with
Arthur H Stockwell Ltd
West Wing Studios
Unit 166, The Mall
Luton, Bedfordshire
ahstockwell.co.uk

Copyright © 2024 William A. Roberts

The right of William A. Roberts to be identified as the author of this work has been asserted in accordance with the Copyright, Designs and Patents Act 1988.

All rights reserved. No reproduction, copy or transmission of this publication may be made without express prior written permission. No paragraph of this publication may be reproduced, copied or transmitted except with express prior written permission or in accordance with the provisions of the Copyright Act 1956 (as amended). Any person who commits any unauthorised act in relation to this publication may be liable to criminal prosecution and civil claims for damage.

The views and opinions expressed herein belong to the author and do not necessarily reflect those of AH Stockwell

Contents

Take Away This Cup 1	Lost. .40
I'll Hold Your Hand. 2	Coloured Skies 41
The Cockroach 3	Murder and Madness. 42
Early Morning. 4	Too Much 43
Are You All Watching? 5	Final Goodbye. 44
Morris Dancers 6	Keeping Watch 45
Morning Ritual 7	Rage 46
Listen to the Wind 8	And They Came Again 47
A Mother's Love. 9	That Same Day 48
Unfortunately 10	Death Knows 49
The Break-Up 11	Love United 50
A Lone Child 12	They've Found You 51
Zero Hour 13	Cherries and Strawberries 52
I Know This Man 14	Only the Ravens Care 53
My Face Stained. 15	She's a Happy Girl. 54
Catching Petals 16	Since the War 55
Too Many Times 17	Neighbour's Home 56
More Than Rainbows. 18	The Crocodile. 57
It's Christmas, My Friends 19	Christmas Time. 58
The Ink in My Pen 20	Happy Without You 59
I Was in the Army 21	Bleach .60
The Oyster. 22	Joining the Furore 61
Hide and Seek. 23	Wanting 62
A Lovers' Dance. 24	Little Jack 63
The Rover 25	No Football 64
You, My Darling. 26	Always 65
Uncontrollable 27	The Moon 66
Going Mad 28	The Child's Name 67
I Live at Home. 29	Broken 68
Make a Statement 30	The Wake 69
A Funny Old World 31	A Right to Cry. 70
Cook .32	They Don't Know 71
I Had a Love. 33	Waking the Dead 72
Too Many Goldfish 34	Voices in My Head 73
After Dark 35	A Million Flies 74
Don't Start Crying 36	The Mice Never Saw a Thing 75
Morning Tea. 37	No One Left 76
The Tears I've Cried. 38	Like a Swan 77
Take Me Back 39	Wake Up 78

Hurry Past 79	Sweet Candy Kisses 119
A Funny Old Thing 80	I'm a Mirror Image 120
Turning 81	A Bundle of Rags 121
Death a Friend 82	The Magic of Young Love 122
The Time Is Nigh 83	Bath Time 123
Shore up the Trenches 84	Tears of a Bugler 124
Flying the Flag 85	Sleep .125
The Days Drag 86	I Mean Well 126
How Many Lives? 87	Let Me Explain 127
Defiant .88	I Need a Doctor 128
Things to Come 89	Just Go 129
Don't Be Sad 90	Sleep? What's Sleep? 130
Memories 91	A Fiery Embrace 131
Joseph 92	Unsightly 132
When We First Met 93	Junkie 133
Going Back 94	Two Small Children 134
Holding Your Ring 95	Two Young Lovers 135
Debbie's Love 96	Tears That Burn 136
A Secret Lover 97	Happy Tears 137
You Blow Me Away 98	Bindweed Around My Heart 138
Sleeping Under the Stars 99	Why Does the Wind Sigh? 139
Please .100	Tesco .140
Dear Maddie 101	To Find a Woman 141
Keeping Warm 102	Catch Me, Gran 142
Today Is Dark 103	Feed Me Sweet Kisses 143
Sewers from Hell 104	Something Cosy 144
No Doubt 105	Too Many Miles 145
A Time for Innocence 106	The Winds of War 146
I'm Waiting for You 108	Summer Days 147
No Way Out 109	She Will Never Be Mine 148
I Can Hear 110	Arms Open Wide 149
A Lifetime Away 111	Take the Tears 150
I Wake Each Morning 112	Tears on a Windowpane 151
The World's on Fire 113	A Lonely Man 152
Yes, My Love 114	Sad As Can Be 154
On the Stove 115	Daylight Is Fading 155
When I See the Sky Crying 116	Happy Fools 156
Another Bleak Day 117	What I Had for Dinner 157
War Has Broken Out 118	Also Available 158

Only the Ravens Care

Take Away This Cup

Take away this cup
I am to taste,

The beatings and abuse that
I'm to endure,

Take away this crown of thorns
and the spitting and whipping,

Then take this cross and burn it in hell.

Take away all these things
so I may live

And in return, on a silver platter,
Man's soul I give to you… Satan.

I'll Hold Your Hand

Let's reach out to each other
across time and space.

Let's go somewhere…
a happy, quiet place.

Let's hold each other
and kiss goodnight.

To wake in each other's arms
when the sun is shining bright.

Dismiss the world
and all those who dwell.

Let's stay this way
until the last knoll of the bell.

And when darkness finally covers the land,

do not fear…

I will hold your delicate hand.

The Cockroach

Inside prison
everything is old
and grey
and dark
and damp
and cold.

Even in summer.
Walls, paint peeling, smell of mould.

Bedclothes damp with urine,
even the light, dim…

and the cockroach
runs and hides in fear.

Early Morning

She woke me,
early hours of the morning,

panic written all over her sleepy, pretty face.

Yawning, I said, "What, babe?"

"Nothing," she replied,
"just thought I'd tell you
I love you…"

Then she rolled over
and went back to sleep.

I got up and made a cup of tea.

Are You All Watching?

Are you all watching?
I'm ready to go.
I have a new bike
(I'll ride real slow).

It's the first time I've ridden it,
don't you see?
(Oh, I hope this bike
isn't too fast for me).

I feel rather nervous
and I've butterflies, you know
(but what will I do
if my bike won't go?).

I'll look rather silly
that's for sure
(perhaps I should store it
'til I'm four?).

Then I'll be a big boy
and can ride all day
(round the garden,
where I must stay).

Morris Dancers

Morris dancers,
a thing from the past
on the village green;
summertime,
opposite the pub.

Mum would take us children
and we'd stand
and watch
and clap.

Dad was in the pub,
perhaps
he looked out the
window.

Pint in one hand,
cigarette
in the other.

And maybe,
just maybe

He smiled.

Morning Ritual

I wake up in the mornings
and wash my sleepy face,
then I reach for my toothbrush
and my toothpaste.

I brush my teeth up and down,
then rinse my mouth all clean
and look into the mirror
to see my smile gleam.

Next, I put the kettle on
for a nice cup of tea,
then open up the curtains
to see what I can see.

The sun is usually smiling
as I greet each new day
and feel his warmth
flowing over me,
washing the last dregs
of sleep away.

Listen to the Wind

When the nights are dark
and there's no place to go
and you're sitting in front of the fire
and you're feeling so low,

when your heart is aching
and tears well in your eyes
and there's a fine mist
covering the skies,

just listen to the wind
gently touching the eaves
and my name being called
softly through gently swaying trees.

Just listen to the wind,
it's travelled far and near;
listen very carefully
and you will hear…

a single tear falling
against your windowpane,
and you will know…

I am home again.

A Mother's Love

They called him INRI, King of the Jews
and nailed him to a tree…

And the north wind blew.

Upon his head
they forced a crown of thorns;
women miscarried,
no children were born.

Men laughed and jeered
as he looked down with pity;
clouds raced overhead,
darkness covered the city.

From his many wounds
warm blood ran free,
down his chilled body
and onto the tree.

His eyes slowly raised skywards,
his life slipping away;
he told his father softly
he would be with him
that day…

and his father's anger
ripped the skies apart,
striking fear into everybody's heart.

Except…

for one lone woman
who knelt beneath his tree,
tears falling silently…

for her son to be free.

Unfortunately

Unfortunately, my darling,
I no longer love you;
I have found another
who loves me in a way
you could never do.

Your tears mean nothing to me,
as mine have had no affect
on you over the years.

Tears I've cried
and you've just laughed.

Thought you had me
in the palm of your hand,

to twist and crush
and then discard at will.

But now you feel what *I* went through.

So, unfortunately my darling,
I have to say…

I no longer love you.

The Break-Up

"Mummy, mummy,
where's the sandman going?"

"Go back to sleep, darling,
mummy's got sewing to do."

"But mummy, mummy,
I saw him there,
bags packed,
walking down the stairs."

A Lone Child

The war's over,
too many dead;
no one sleeps
in their beds.

Hospitals once full,
now desolate and rubble.

So much blood running,
making puddles
thick and sticky.

And all the while,
the raven eats
her fill of meat,

rancid, stinking,
no mean feat…

but there are many bodies left to the wild.

And the only sound is the mournful cry…

of a lone child.

Zero Hour

Zero hour,
guns ablaze,
fear…

Cold steel fingers
shred and tear.

Grenades exploding,
beaches eroding.

Machine-gun madness,
bullets ripping
and piercing
like so many
angry bees.

Let death come
instantly,
please.

Mortar shells plop,
shower of sand;
bodies already dead
somersault through the air.

Jigsaw pieces
of human flesh,

bone and sinew,
raw angry meat,

blood and sand,
blinding eyes…

as darkness covers
clear blue skies.

I Know This Man

I know this man
who's nailed
to the tree.

He looks down
so pitifully;
his eyes hold
such sorrow for…

the morrow.

Because
he knows Man
is heading for
a fall.

And they don't know
and they can't see
Satan

in the shadows, waiting patiently.

My Face Stained

My face is stained,
blood in my stubble;
dirt under my nails
through fighting in rubble.

The stench of death is everywhere
but I'm too afraid to care;
just let me live one more day,
on bended knees I pray.

But God doesn't answer,
the Boche are here;
I feel so sick in my stomach
through worry and fear.

Let a bullet find me
quick and clean,
no time for pain.

Just beautiful dreams
in somewhere green;
poppies and roses a sight to be seen.

But death doesn't come my way today
and now we're on the run
after the Boche.

Tomorrow they'll be back, stronger than before.

Is the whole world really at war?

Catching Petals

Catch the delicate petals of a rose
should the cold winter winds blow.

Catch the stars should they fall
and listen to a lone loon call.

Listen to the skies cry in pain
as it gives birth to itself again,

ripping and tearing itself apart.

War is here my friends.
This is the start… and it's only going to get worse.

Too Many Times

Too many times
I've shot my gun
in the fields
just for fun.

Rabbits,
pheasants,
hares,
who cares?

Not me.

At war now,

different field,
bigger gun.

No hares,
rabbits,
nor pheasants.

Just endless lines
of the Hun.

More Than Rainbows

I hold a kaleidoscope
of colours in my palm,
so sparkling,
so pretty,
spreading up my arm
and into my eyes.

So much more beautiful
than all the rainbows in the skies.

And like the fires of hell,
fiery and red,

I cut your throat
and your blood:
just as red.

It's Christmas, My Friends

Bring out the
whiskey, wine and beer;

cook the turkey,
the gang's all here.

Hollering and laughing,
music a-blare,

kids running around…
no one cares.

It's Christmas, my friends;
cards to send

and many broken hearts to mend…
except mine.

You've been gone a year today;
I can't find the words I'd like to say.

My heart's in pieces,
torn apart.

I kneel at your graveside
and sob my heart out.

Oh, how I miss you, my darling.

The Ink in My Pen

The ink in my pen—
black, thick & stubborn—

just would not write,
try as I might.

Gently scratch
across the page…

Nothing.

Try again and again,
losing patience.

Throw it across the room,
sit, puffing and panting.

Looking at it
looking at me.

Get up and go over,
bend down and pick it up,

Look at it…
and then lovingly snap the bloody thing in two.

I Was in the Army

I was in the army,
the army of the dead;
but they got fed up when I wet the bed.

"No, no," they cried,
pointing their bony fingers
at my bony chest.

"Can't rest?" I ask,
more of a plea,
"No, no, no, just go away, pissy."

So here I am, walking alone
through the darkness
and past my old home.

They're long since gone,
the wife and kids;
no one around

No one to see me lying in bed and pissing so happily.

The Oyster

And the oyster,
overcome with despair,

turned slowly,
constantly in its shell.

And all the while,
life carried on,
oblivious to its plight.

A single half-choked sob
escaped from the troubled creature,
only to be lost in the vastness of time.

Hide and Seek

"Come out, come out,
wherever you are!"
and the child cowers with fear.

A single sob escapes
and shatters the silence,

Tears fall freely
as a small heart
beats frantically
inside a tiny chest.

Footsteps,
heavy, slow, but near.

Red-rimmed eyes,
puffy, swollen with tears.

The hammer,
hard, new, heavy and shiny;

as yet clean and innocent—

as innocent as the child.

Found you!

And the face
a familiar face,
daddy's face.

And the hammer
falling,
falling,
falling,

again and again.

A Lovers' Dance

Hand in hand,
toe to toe,
around the dance floor
the lovers go.

Stealing shy glances,
cheeks all aglow,
hands tightening slightly
as around they go.

Eyelashes a-flutter,
hearts in tune,
still faster and faster
they twirl around the room.

Music becoming distant,
lights going dim
and in each other's eyes
the young lovers swim.

The Rover

Up and over
she came from Dover
and she drove
an old Rover.

The field was in clover
the first time we kissed;
my heart missed
and I took a risk and married her.

And so many years ago
(twenty-seven don't you know)!
We still only have eyes for each other
and the Rover has turned to rust.

You, My Darling

You have a guilty face, my dear.
Where do you go when you're not here?

Have you a lover,
or just fed up with me?

Why can't you just tell me true?
I can no longer put up with you.

Lies and deceit
all the time;

a once-loving heart
now crushed and bound.

The knife in my hand
your soft flesh has found,

and now on the ground
silence reigns
and you, my darling… and you.

Uncontrollable

Uncontrollably true
the way I loved you;
sweet kisses
no more.

Walk out the door
and my life,
no longer mine.

I dine alone at home;
so quiet without you,
no clue as to where you've gone.

All I have is a blood-smeared kiss
and a knife stained with blood…

your blood.

Going Mad

The ship,
navigating the river
slowly, slowly,
inch by inch.

Engines on slow,
onwards,
forwards,
and then…

she moors safe and sound.

That's how my life
is navigating life's twists
and turns;
slowly, slowly,
inch by inch.

It's dark
and I feel my way like a blind man.
I have no place to moor,
no place that's safe and sound.

I'm to forever stumble,
hands outstretched,
fumbling,
stumbling
and going…

mad.

I Live at Home

I live at home
with some of my family;
I have plenty of friends,
all this love and kindness
aimed at me.

but…

I'm still lonely,
so very lonely,
to the point of being sick
and suicidal.
I won't be missed.

Will I?

Make a Statement

Make a statement,
the police said;
tell us how you found
your wife dead.

So, I thought for a while
and then I smiled and said
I came home from work
and she was still alive…

until I took my hammer
and smashed in her head.
That's when I found her lifeless
and dead

I said, smugly.

A Funny Old World

It's a funny old world
and that much we know;
flowers that have grown
now return to seed.

Trees stretch
to the point of splitting apart;
seas dry and turn to land;
mountains freeze and shatter.

And the sky, once blue,
now blacker than night,
and the sun much too heavy
to suspend up high…

falls…

screaming
and explodes
on the ground.

Cook

Cook
and the family will eat.

Cook
and her meat so sweet.

Cook
and her body laid bare.

Cook
and there's enough there.

Cook
and we share

getting rid of her bones.

I Had a Love

Once I had a love
for the whole world to see;
beauty beyond compare,
she was perfect for me.

We would laugh and cry
all at the same time;
life was ours,
beautiful sunshine.

Then *he* came along
and stole her from me;
broke my heart,
so lonely.

And I know today
I will never find
someone else to laugh and cry
in sunshine.

Alone today
and forever more
since you left
and walked out the door.

Too Many Goldfish

Too many goldfish,
not enough room.
I look into their little glass bowl.

Huddled together,
nowhere to go,
they look so sad;
it's more than I can stand.

There's not enough room.
Go and get the spoon,
give them a bloody good stir;
that's livened the little sods up.

Look at them swirl,
like being on the waltzer
up at the fair.

After Dark

She comes to me
after dark
in the inky blackness
of the night.

Like a spark
she shines bright,
and her passion
sustains me all through the night.

And with the dawn
I stretch and yawn
with only the scent
of her perfume
on the pillow
to show where's she been.

And I lie in the gloom
looking into nothing
and smile.

Don't Start Crying

Don't start crying;
I've had enough of your lying.
Days and years you've brought me to tears…
but not anymore.

Sure, I still love you—
and that's a fact.
When we married,
we made a pact
to love each other for all time.

But I was blind
as you ran around
and now I've found
all these men,
way back then.

So forgive me my darling,
I've had enough of your lying.
And as for your crying,
it means nothing to me anymore.

Morning Tea

I'd like to find a woman,
someone to share my life.
Maybe in time we'd love each other
and she would become my wife,
happy ever after and all of that.

We'd have a reception,
a place to hang my hat.
Each morning I'd awake,
stretch and yawn
and look at her,
my little fawn.

I'd kiss her nose
once or twice;
she'd open her eyes
and say that's nice.

Then I'd go in the kitchen
and make a brew,
a cup of tea for me
and a cup of tea for you.

The Tears I've Cried

Eight years ago
I was happy as can be,
living with my girl
down by the sea.

We would laugh
and joke and poke fun of each other.

The days were ours for the taking;
everyone else was left forsaking.

We didn't care, it was just us;
we didn't moan, grumble or fuss.

And then you were gone.
Back in my arms is where you belong,
but it cannot be;
you've been taken from me.

With the tears I have cried,
all I do now is kneel by your side.

The hole in which you now lie,
so long and so wide,
is nearly full
with the tears I have cried.

Take Me Back

Take me back,
kiss me no more,
let me sleep
on the cold, hard wooden floor.

Score your lovers
one to ninety more,
carry on just as you have before.

Just let me be near you,
ease my pain
and I'll never argue with you again.

Lost

Stripped and beaten
all through the night,
a crown of thorns didn't look right.

Blood running down,
blurring his sight,
nailed to a tree
for the whole world to see.

And the devil sat there,
smirking at the pain
of this man,

but was too much
of a coward
to come out and say,
"All of mankind,
you have lost today."

Coloured Skies

And the raven,
a craven liar,
said last night
there was no fire.

But in the cold light of day
saw a city, once gay,
now lying in a heap of rubble.

Muddle through
to find anyone alive.

And in the distance,
mushrooms filling
the strangely-coloured skies.

Murder and Madness

A lifetime away
and yet so near.

Dead are crying;
they shed no tear.

Tossing in their tombs,
they fight to breathe.

Eyes now blind,
seeing into man's black heart.

Depart…

No, we stay as one,
bury us both under autumn sun.

Nothing too harsh,
it's out of play.

Murder and madness
on the menu today.

Too Much

There's too much going on
for me to be afraid.

War and disease,
hunger and drought;
what have I to gripe about?

Two voices raging
inside my head

while men, women and children
are lying dead.

Who am I to whinge and whine?
Those poor people
would swap their lives for mine
any time.

I know all this,
yet still I long
for death to come.

I'm not selfish
or ungrateful,
I just want to die.

So let's get on with it.

Final Goodbye

It's come round
all too quick.
I knew you'd leave me,
but I still feel sick.

What will I do
once you are gone?
I wish to God
I knew what I'd done wrong.

Yet you say you love me
and I set your heart on fire;
I know you all too well,
you're nothing but a liar.

I can't keep you here
no matter how I try,
so this really is our final goodbye.

Keeping Watch

"Let's count the stars
before we die,"
These words that she spoke
still make me cry.

We were so in love,
the world at our feet;
life was good
and she so sweet.

But time passes
and we grow old;
the autumn sun lets in the cold
and the stars in the sky
twinkle down keeping watch over you,

deep in the ground.

Rage

And God shook with rage,
and man trembled with fear;
the heavens were ripped apart
and lightning streaked across the skies.

Everything was dark.
The sound of God's booming voice:
"Adam," he shouted,
"you had a choice. Why go against what I say?
You're banished from Eden this very day."

And Eve came along,
sassy in her ways,
and God cursed her
for the rest of her days.

So out of Eden they went,
hand in hand
into a barren land
and a hostile world.

And They Came Again

A thousand screaming men
tearing down the hill
through the trees
and fields
to the front line.

Wait, we are told,
wait a little longer…
and then
open fire.
And we do,
but have no ammo.

And as they run
across the land
we rush out.

Hand to hand
Fighting,
it's harsh,
brutal,
sickening.

The wounded are stamped upon
along with the dead,
ground no longer brown,
now it runs red.

And when the fighting
is over and done,
we push back the enemy
back to where they came.

And with the setting of the sun
so they come again,
and again
and again.

That Same Day

Like a cork
bobbing on the waves of the sea,
the ocean seems to beckon me.

No one around,
no one to see,
as I give myself to the cold cruel sea.

With arms opened wide,
she invites me to come inside.

But she lied; when I died
she tossed me aside,
and though I cried and begged her to stay,
she moved onto another lover that very same day.

Death Knows

Your smile
just trickles
and drips
to the floor.

Your eyes,
burning coals,
set fire to my soul.

Your kisses magic
and taste of death.

You take my soul
when you take my breath,

leaving me icy cold.
Even the grave tries to hold onto you.

Even death has fallen for you
and knows pain of heart when you leave.

Love United

Love united;
two hearts
hold and caress,
feeling happy and content.

Love to last beyond
and above life itself.

But that was then;
this is now,
and the love we shared
has now gone sour.

Somehow you got bored
and went away,
leaving me here
with nothing to say.

They've Found You

She's cold to the touch,
but I love her so much
and would do anything
to keep her near.

The fear of losing her
day by day
is an ache in my heart
that won't go away.

They'll find you soon
in the spare room,
grey, bloated and green.

And the flies are many,
feeding off you;
their buzzing is real,
the smell, evil…

and makes me want to be sick;
got to be quick.

They're breaking down the door,
seems they've found you after all.

Cherries and Strawberries

There's so much going on.
One of us must be wrong,
and laughter is just a thing of the past.

Kisses are sweet
as our lips meet;
cherries and strawberries
come to mind.

But now you're no more,
lying crumpled on the floor
with nothing much to say.

My world is grey,
I'd love you to stay
but the smell is overpowering.

I'll bury you deep
so you can sleep
and leave those men alone…

Just for once.

Only the Ravens Care

For the last five days
the ocean waves have crashed ashore.

And there's more to come:
the sounds of guns
and bombs exploding;
beaches folding in on themselves.

Bodies here
and bodies there;

this, my friend, is warfare.

And it's only the ravens who care,
as they peck the eyes of the dead.

She's a Happy Girl

She was a happy girl,
a quiet girl,
a silent girl,
a shy girl
when she was young.

Now she has grown
and is a beauty to see;
I'm in love with her
and she with me.

We have children of our own;
we worked hard
and had a lovely home.

I can't wish for any more from this life;
just sweet kisses from my lovely wife.

Since the War

And the ocean's black
and the fish are no more;
trees are all dying
since the start of the war.

Children screaming
out with pain;
bombers dropping
death again.

Is nowhere safe for us to go?
Hide away in some hole,
but the bombs are many,
destroying all.

Listen… you can hear them whistling
as they fall.
And I'm scared stiff.

Neighbour's Home

Neighbour's home;
don't know where he's been.
Been gone all day,
nothing much to say.

Let them be,
if they leave *me* alone.

Sit here looking
out the window.
I see them;
they don't see me.

That's how I like it.
He'll be gone tomorrow.

Thank God.

The Crocodile

And the crocodile
looked up from his mud hole
and soerly seen a tree
so green.

And the bison had left
a long time ago.

His belly was rumbling
and making a noise;
he wants to eat

girl or boy,
and the pheasant was coy.

The lion roared
and the crocodile got bored
and fell asleep in the mud.

Christmas Time

And so, Christmas time has come again.
All the turkeys have been slain;
veggies in the pot
boiling away,
nice and hot.

Decorations cover the tree;
friends and family
come by to see.

The turkey's cooked,
the veg is too.

Seated around the table…
Happy Christmas to all of you.

Happy Without You

Let me know
before you go
and I'll put out
the banners and flags.

Dress yourself warm;
there's going to be a storm
and I don't want you to catch a chill.

Another pill?
You've had so many.
Let me be;
killing yourself
won't worry me.

I want you gone
either way;
you can walk
or they'll carry you away.

The choice is yours
and yours alone.
Go find some place to make your home.
To be honest, I'm quite happy here
without you.

Bleach

I drank a bottle
of bleach
just to teach
myself a lesson.

These voices
in my head,
screaming at me
to kill you dead,

suffocate you in bed,
but I just can't do it.
You've done nothing wrong,
except
the lack of your love towards me.

It was the bleach, I see,
drinking it down in one go;
but still these voices just won't go.

So here I am now,
many years down the line;
you left me when you said
I was a swine.
That's fine.

But at least you're still alive,
which is more than I can say for me.

Joining the Furore

Way, way back,
when Germany went to war,
nearly every country in the world
joined in the furore.

And before you knew it,
the dead were lying piled on the floor.

Many, many more were injured or maimed,
and when the atom bombs were sent to fly,
those murderous mushrooms bloomed in the sky.

Why?

Because it was a new toy
that they wanted to play with
and this, their excuses.

I hope they can sleep at night,
because I can't.

Wanting

Too many times
I've wanted to die.
No, *longed* to die.

Why?

Because I feel
I'm a burden to life;
no children,
no wife.

Just me on my own—
apart from those inside my head.
Day after day,
night after night.

Smash my head
against the wall;
self-harm severely…
but that's not all.

Pills by my side,
bright sharp razor too.

One of these days,
I'll show you.

Little Jack

Little Jack Horner
was made to sit in the corner
for pulling Becky's hair.

The punishment fair,
but little Jack didn't care.
And when another girl walked by,
he pulled her hair and made her cry.

No Football

The three wise men
were not wise at all:
bringing gold,
frankincense
and myrrh…

but no football.

How could Jesus
make the national team?

Sorry people, it's just a dream.

With Christ on our side
we could beat them.

Pity, back then
there was no football.

Always

Why is the world
round and not flat?

Why is a dog
not like a cat?

Why is a scarf
not like a hat?

And why are you
so wild and free?

Is it because of me?

And why do your lovers
number fifty-two?

Although I'm leaving,
I'll always love you.

The Moon

The moon,
pale,
watery;

and the stars
like dead fish
eyes in the sky;

and your lips,
chapped and cold;
they hold no warmth for me.
I have forgotten you easily
from my mind,

and I wait patiently
each day
for them to find your body
somewhere on the heath.

The Child's Name

And Mother Earth
is giving birth
to a terror
never seen before.

The pain she feels
as she splits and tears
is so much more
than man.

This is corruption,
murder
and death,

and Mother Earth
is taking her last breath.
And all for what?

There is no more.

This child's name is…
NUCLEAR WAR!

Broken

Broken
and tomorrow
not yet here;
a lifetime to wait…
and the night draws on.

And the moth,
skittish
and frail,
beating itself futile
again and again
against the electric light bulb.

The Wake

They call it a wake,
sitting up all night
with the dead.

Paying respect,
showing love,
eating and drinking,
sharing stories—
some funny,
others sad.

Everyone has kind words;
nothing bad
would be tolerated.

The night moves swiftly;
soon the day breaks.
Moon and stars—
their time to go,
relieved from their vigil.

The hearse pulls up;
time for the funeral.
Looking up at the sky…
going to be a lovely day.

A Right to Cry

The dandelion
has forgotten to roar,

the clover is nothing
but a bore.

The buttercup
so pretty to see,

the grass
so pleasant.

And the willow looks down,
tears in her eyes.

Cherry blossom fills the skies,
so tender and gentle,

Not like those bombers, riding high,
now everything has a right to cry.

They Don't Know

Why scream with pain?
He'll only do it all over again.

A bullet in the brain is quick.

Blood running red
and thick
and slick,
in pools and puddles.

Everyone's muddled.

War, they say;
a hero's death.
But in reality
death's very breath
is the only breath
you'll know,
hiding in a foxhole.

Poor, poor souls.

Back in Blighty
they don't know the suffering and fear,
not like our boys dying over here.

Waking the Dead

A coffin
is a home for one,
dark as dark;
there is no sun.

Just enough room
to lie and sleep,
under the ground
so so deep.

Death is there
in the graveyard,
making sure you stay where you are;
although he goes,
he's never far.

And the sound
of a car back-firing
in the distance
is enough
to wake the dead.

Voices in My Head

Voices in my head,
dark and deep,
screaming so loud,
unable to sleep.

Let the devil come
and take my soul;
bury me deep
in a hole.

Maggots and worms
eat my flesh.

No more voices,
no more screaming;
never again
will I be dreaming.

Leave me to rot
in my grave.

My soul so tainted
it cannot be saved;
let me die
with dignity.

A Million Flies

Bodies rotting,
piled high;
the buzzing sound
of a million flies.

These little creatures
on your face and hair;
they might be small
but don't like to share.

Slowly, slowly,
they eat their way
through a multitude of corpses
every day.

The Mice Never Saw a Thing

Mumbling,
bumbling,
fumbling
my way through life.

Carve the turkey
with a knife,
then turn it on your wayward wife.
Carve her thinly,
slice by slice.

And the three blind mice
never saw a thing.

No One Left

Everything is jumbled,
nothing the same.
It's man that's done it;
it's him to blame.

I don't know
what he was thinking;
now corpses lie about, stinking.

The rats and ravens
are having their fill;
the eyes of the dead, tasty still.

Oh, what a thrill, this war.
Must get together
and have one more…

but there is no one left to fight.

Like a Swan

I'm like a swan
out on the lake,
gently bobbing up and down
on the small waves
the breeze makes.

On the surface
I look so majestic and serene,
but under the water
it's frantic,
almost a nightmare.

Paddling, paddling,
with nowhere to go,
under the water,
going so slow.

Smiling at the people
up on shore,
I wanted to scream—
I can't take any more.

Wake Up

*Wake up, wake up,
you're having a nightmare.*

I'm living a nightmare
and you don't care.

*Share your thoughts
and voices with me.*

You wouldn't cope, believe me.

*Let me try to understand;
here, take my outstretched hand.*

What can you do?
Pray, tell me please.
These voices are bringing me
down to my knees.

*Don't give up,
hold on tight.*

I can't do it any more,
I have no fight.

*What are you doing
with that razor so bright
against your wrist so pale tonight?*

Hurry Past

Restaurant,
well-known place,
average price
for a meal.

Drinking, eating,
having fun.

Laughter and squeals
reverberate
around the room.

Tipping generously
as they leave,
collars up,
shut out the rain.

Not a glance at the young woman
by the door,
feeling faint,
not eaten for three days now.

Those that see her
say loud enough for her to hear,
"dirty cow
what's she doing here?"

And her stomach rumbles
and tears fall free;
years ago, she belonged to me.

I see her. Head lowered, I hurry past.

A Funny Old Thing

Humour…
what is humour?
People talk about it;
some even partake
and still others don't know.

But… it's strange,
when spoken of
most people
snigger,
chortle,
or just laugh.

It's one of those things
that has for the most part
the same effect.

If asked about it
I wouldn't have an explanation,
except to say… it' s a funny old thing.

Turning

I don't know
what I'm doing
or saying;
my head,
my brain,
turning in on itself.

Why, though?
Surely, if it harms me
then it harms them.

I don't understand;
no one likes
pain,
suffering,
going through life longing for death.
But that's what I do.

Death a Friend

For those who don't know,
death is a friend.
Nothing to be scared of;
he's there for all of us,
one way or another

At the end of your life
when light turns black,
he'll come and sit with you
with his scythe and sack.

He will hold your hand,
give comfort to you,
and when it's time for you to go,
he will lift your spirit ever so gently
and take you to a place of milk and honey.

You know… I've been there before.

The Time Is Nigh

The time is nigh,
the time is here;
it's the end of
mankind's era.

The devil's won—
he's lied, with ease.

No time now
to say thank you
or please.

Long queues of the dead,
winding their way into hell;
burning souls, the only smell.

And the days are dark,
with flashes of red smoke
billowing higher from the burning dead.

Shore up the Trenches

Shore up the trenches;
wood,
tin,
whatever is at hand.

Do it quickly, quietly;
the enemy are doing the same
just a few metres away.

It's hard work,
almost impossible,
while carrying a rifle
and several grenades.

And all for what?
A few feet of barren land
that no one wants or cares for.

Flying the Flag

Fly the flag,
we're going to war!
And there are many more

young men
signing away their youth,
so uncouth.

Think it's romantic,
such a laugh.

Wake and find yourself
dead in the bath,
water now cold
and red and congealed.

The Days Drag

The days drag;
there's no colour to my life,
not any more.

I've forgotten
how to laugh,
to smile.
My heart hangs heavy in my chest,
my blood pounds in my ears.

And tears…
so many tears,
warm and salty.

And death—
how I long to be with you.
The pain I'm feeling,
you will never know.

How Many Lives?

How many lives
must we lose?
It's war we choose
over peace.

So much easier
to burn and die.

Bombers fill the beautiful skies
and no one asks the question,
"what for?"

Why do men
go to war
and fight an enemy new,

laying down their lives?
Women too.

And all for what?
A devastated earth
and no one now left
to ask the question,

"Why do we do it; what's it all for?"

Defiant

And God looked at man
and said
what have you done?

And man, sick with fear,
trembled in the sight of the Lord
and fell to his knees.

And woman,
hands on hips,
looked defiantly at God

…and sniggered.

Things to Come

And so it was,
man and his wife
were cast out of Eden
for disobeying God.

The serpent
was joyous
and slid away
into the shadows,
happily, contentedly
and excitedly at what was to come.

Don't Be Sad

I'm sorry mother,
I went to war
like so many others
who have gone before.

The guns are quiet;
there's a stillness
over the land.

I'm lying,
dying,
but I'm not alone.

Death is here
to take me home.

Not with you,
mother dear;
never again will I see
your loving smile.

Death has taken my hand.
I'll be gone in a while.

Forgive me mother,
I'm not really bad;
it's this war.

Please, don't be sad.

Memories

Memories of my grandfather.
Old,
grey whiskers,
thin,
bed-ridden,
oxygen mask,
smelling of death
and urine.

Joseph

Joseph
the forgotten one,
stepfather of the holy one;
you married his mother
though she was with child.

Loving her,
you weren't wild.

You brought the Christ
up to be good,
and, this laid down,
Christ understood.

Working with his hands
and with you at his side,
Jesus grew up
with nothing to hide.

And when they beat him
and hung him high,
you looked up at him
and asked through teary eyes
this simple question… *please tell me why?*

When We First Met

When we first met
and I kissed your ruby red lips,

and felt the gentle sway
of your hips,

I gave you my heart
and my soul.

You thanked me so much—
and buried them in a hole,

along with all the others.

Going Back

Don't worry about me,
it's nothing to you.
Leave if you're going,
if that's what you want to do.

No self-pity,
no tears feigning love;
you'll be judged one day
by him up above.

So, now you've come
and passed through my life,
I think it's time
I went back to my wife…

Don't you?

Holding Your Ring

I never thought
I was a jealous man;
thought I had you
in the palm of my hand…

'til last night,
when I saw you together.

I could do nothing but walk away,
and in the cold light of day
you've packed your things
and have gone your way.

My fault, really.

I couldn't bring myself
to beg you to stay;
begging isn't one of my things.

So I sit here alone,
holding your wedding ring
in the dark…

where my tears go unnoticed.

Debbie's Love

She loved me,
but I loved another;
she told me
there would be no other.

The place in her heart
was for me alone
and she would wait
for as long as it would take.

The girl I loved
didn't return my feelings,
and my heart would take
a whole lot of healing.

But Debbie is there,
waiting for me.

If only I could see;
if I wasn't so blind,
I'd take Debbie by the hand
and make her mine.

A Secret Lover

And out of the darkness
Eve appeared,
looked at man
and sneered.

Man was besotted
with the beautiful Eve;
followed her everywhere,
he just would not leave.

She picked an apple
from off the tree,
a bite for you
and a bite for me.

And man ate the apple
so happily.

When God cried out,
"What have you done?"
Eve turned and said,
"It was only fun."

Man was on his toes;
he was about to leave,
when God said to man,
"I'm going to make
your life a misery…

you'd better believe me."

And Eve walked away,
pleased with the day
and met her lover in secret…

and it's been that way ever since.

You Blow Me Away

You blow me away
when your kisses stray,
and another tastes your lips
so sweet.

But what can I do?
I'm in love with you,
but you can't be true—
not for one day.

So I'm going away;
I have no idea
where I'll stay.

Don't say a thing;
keep your wedding ring
and everything in our home—
I'd rather be alone.

A covering of stars
to light my way;
I know I'll be happy after today.

So I'll say goodbye
and wish you well;
whatever happens
you'll always be…

my little Tinker Bell!

Sleeping Under the Stars

"I'm all alone,"
she said on the phone
and Jack next door
came round.

I was out for a while
and returned with a smile,
not expecting this:
Jack and my wife sharing a passionate kiss.

She saw me there
and I truly swear
she had a smirk
on her pretty face.

I turned around
and walked out the door,
and swore I'd never take her back again;
the pain I felt was too much to bear.

Now I sleep
under skies and stars.
It could have easily
been sleeping behind iron bars.

But the stars keep silent watch
as I sleep at night,
and the sun is there in the morning light…

comforting me.

Please

I escaped yesterday
from a life of sin;
open the door
and let me in.

I beg and plead,
it's loving I need;
some place away
where I can lead
a happy normal life.

I have no children,
I have no wife;
I used to…
until I killed them
with the steak knife.

So you see,
I escaped yesterday
from a life of sin;
please open the door
and welcome me in.

Dear Maddie

Dear… dear Maddie—
you're going to marry a baddie.

Run, dear Maddie, run—
while the sun is high in the sky.

Hide, Maddie, hide—
the devil wants you for his bride.

Maddie, Maddie… please come here—
the devil is so very near.

Cry, Maddie, cry—
shed a tear;
the devil's at the door…

the devil's here!

Keeping Warm

The weather's ferocious,
the blizzard is harsh;
snow and ice
thick on the ground.

People huddled together
trying to keep warm;
these poor wretches
are all that's left.

The war of all wars has come
and Mother Earth is at the end of her tether.
She's had enough of man
and she's making it known.

The weather's ferocious,
the blizzard's harsh;
snow and ice
feel like shards of glass.

Today Is Dark

And today is dark

No light…

No warmth…

And the flowers
curl up on themselves
as if to hide from the bombers
as they drop their load,
and devastation covers the land.

Sewers from Hell

And out from the sewers of hell
a form emerged…

and awoke…

and grew…

and this form knew evil
and the devil's ways.

And this form was…

man.

No Doubt

I feel you there
at the bottom
where I stare,
and know
I will never be free.

Just behind my eyes
I silently cry.

And the bartender asks for money.

Sunny days ahead;
I've not been fed
from the grace
that comes from
your very soul.

Leave it to me
and I will see
if I've done anything wrong.

I doubt it…

but I'll look anyway.

A Time for Innocence

A young boy stands
as motionless
as a sentinel.

Small hands
gripped tightly around
a bamboo cane
of a fishing net;

head slightly downcast.
And the tip
of a small pink glistening tongue
pokes from the corner of his mouth.

Blue eyes aflame
with excitement—
concentration,
transfixed,
unblinking…

As if by staring hard enough,
the murky stream waters
that tug gently at
fire-engine red
wellington boots

would magically
begin to clarify,
revealing all—
and all to be caught.

The fact that life
is extinct
in these murky waters
doesn't enter the child's mind.

After all…

he has his net,
a stream,
and time…

plenty of time!

I'm Waiting for You

I'm waiting for you
to come and go,
my heart beating ever so slow.

The screams of the dead
sweet music to my ears;
acid, acid, acid for tears.

People running
fearing me so;
running, running
with nowhere to go

Hide under the table,
hide under the bed;
I will soon find you
and cut off your head.

(Goodnight my darling, sweet dreams).

No Way Out

In the deep
dark
recesses
of my mind,

evil lives.

I hear it
and feel it—
scratching,
clawing,
screaming;

bouncing off
the walls of my mind.
No respite,
no reprieve,
not for a moment.

Constant,
constant,
day and night.

People say hell
is all in the mind.

Well, this much I know—
they're bloody right there.

And if not,
then the real hell
can't be any worse
than living with
these voices in my head.

Day after day,
year after year—
and there's no way out
for me.

I Can Hear

I can hear them talking
in the other room.
No room for me though,
left out in the cold.

I hear their laughter
and jovial banter,
and I sit alone
and wonder why.

Why do I keep going?
What's the use?
I can hear them now,
the doctors and nurses
just outside my door.

My room's padded
and my jacket
does up at the back.

No room to move.

They said they'd untie it soon – can't wait!

A Lifetime Away

Life—
what *is* life?

Most people enjoy life, embrace it each day.

It makes them happy;
they feel alive.
When asked what they think of life,
they will say it's far too short

Ask me—
and I will say it's far too long.

When you're waiting… no, *longing*
for death to come,
it's a lifetime away.

I Wake Each Morning

I wake each morning
to catch the first rays of light,
happy and content.

But then…

all too soon
the afternoon is here,
and with it
the terrors start.

Knowing the night,
the unbreakable night,

is a place where
nightmares plague me.

Cold sweats
and lack of sleep;
I have no control
over the dreams I'm in.

Sometimes I shake
and look around my room
just to make sure
I'm still alone.

And then…

I wake in the morning
and catch the first rays of light.
And with the dawn,
the night takes flight and runs away and hides.

Bloody coward.

The World's on Fire

The world's on fire;
we've pushed the earth
right to the wire.

Bullets and bombs,
planes and tanks,

people dying—
they get no thanks.

Children screaming
out with pain,

sky awash with acid rain.

Towns razed to the ground…
and the only sound
is that of the raven,

crying tears of desperation.

Yes, My Love

Yes, my love;
I know—
I fully agree,
you set the agenda.

And I'll go down the pub
and go on a bender.

Your words are harsh
and blistering.

I just need a couple of pints—
just a few beers.

Yes, my love,
I'm all ears.

And pissed off
with your constant nagging
and moaning.

For Christ's sake, give me a break, please.

On the Stove

I'm at that stage
in life
where I want a wife.

But they fear
the knife
in my hand.

Make a stand
and cut her again.

The pain she feels
excites me more
than she will ever know.

Just keep looking…
while the last one is cooking nicely
on the stove.

When I See the Sky Crying

When I see the sky crying
across all the land,
I wish you were near me
to take my cold hand.

I wish you were near me
to hold me tight,
to whisper sweet nothings
through these long, lonely nights.

When I see the sky crying
and the day filled with pain,
it matches the aching
my heart feels again.

The longing and needing
for you to be near;
I love you my darling,
I think that is clear.

So let the sky cry
and mourn the cold day;
my love for you, darling,
is never far away.

Another Bleak Day

It's raining outside,
the sky dull and grey;
it looks as inviting
as a stagnant pond.

No wonder it's crying.

And the wind seems
to have taken on the form
of a mischievous child,

teasing and tormenting
the little drops of water
as they laboriously struggle
to meet their journey's end.

And me…

I just sit here
looking out of a barred window,
watching with eyes
that do not see.

No wonder I'm crying.

War Has Broken Out

There's so much going on;

won't be long.

Ships and planes,
tanks and guns,
all beautifully made—

but deadly.

Made to kill.

And all the dead
and those dying
know the rules:
lie down quietly,
peacefully,
comfortably
…and die.

Sweet Candy Kisses

Soft moonlight kisses
that are candy sweet
from lips that are burning
with love's own heat.

So warm and inviting
you hunger for more,
and each new kiss
tastes sweeter than the ones before.

Hands that are warm
and yearn to caress,
but which tremble slightly
as you hold your sweetness.

Feeling her melting
into your arms as you embrace;
gazing at the beauty
that is there on her face.

Loving eyes that sparkle
in the light from bright stars in the sky
enhance the tears of happiness
that your sweetheart now cries.

Cherishing each moment
as you hold her so tight,
and knowing there's magic
in this cool moonlit night.

Two hearts that are beating
like soft falling rain,
as two lips gently steal
sweet candy kisses again.

I'm a Mirror Image

I'm a mirror image of myself
but I'm confused.

Am I the one looking in
at my reflection
or the one looking out?

I don't know
which one of us
is real, or who is the reflection.

If *I'm* real then
where does my image go
when I walk away from the mirror?

Am *I* living or is *he*?
Or are we all just mirror images
in a world made of mirrors?

A Bundle of Rags

Christmas time; a time for
happiness,
smiles,
laughter.

For most.

Gifts exchanged,
gratitude from all,

except…

for the bundle of dirty rags,
shivering unseen,
huddled tight
against the cold damp wall
on the damp cold pavement.

The Magic of Young Love

Lullabies sung softly,
kisses warm and light;
stars shining brightly
high in the heavens that night.

The magic of young love
slowly opens like a rose
and the taste of your first kiss
you wish would never go.

Young hearts flying together,
so high and carefree,
and only love for each other
these two hearts can see.

Happiness and excitement
and laughter galore,
wishing this precious moment
could last forever more.

The feeling of nervousness
and a million butterflies
as your sweetheart gazes tenderly
into your own loving eyes.

Two hearts beating faster,
hands trembling slight;
two lips gently kissing
under soft pale moonlight.

And the sounds of a lullaby
are carried as gentle as a sigh,
for two hearts slowly rising
to forever sparkle in the sky.

Bath Time

Bath time again…
and the acid eats
through flesh and bone;
no trace is left.

And all the while
the yellow plastic duck watches
with uncaring,
unblinking eyes.

Tears of a Bugler

Out across a dew-kissed field,
the mournful cry of a bugle
carries far and wide.

Clouds turn their tear-swollen faces away
as they slowly, silently pass the lone bugler by.

And as the dull, saddened sun
respectfully bows its head,
a single tear falls
from red-rimmed eyes.

The gentle hand of the autumn wind
carries the bugler's tears,
gently laying them to rest
amongst the multi-coloured leaves
that lay scattered beneath
the bare-limbed trees

like the shards of a broken rainbow.

Sleep

The wife's gone to bed;
said she's tired,
needs sleep.

Wish I could sleep—
tired all day;
no nightmares though.

Don't worry about the night falling.

Used to.
Dreaded it;
made me ill.
Not anymore.

Trouble is, where I've had
so many bad nights over the years,
my body clock wakes me;
early hours of the morning.

Wife's not amused, needs her sleep.

I Mean Well

The forest
with its many wonders
lies sprawled as far as the eye can see.

Trees, of course;
but the animals
that lie beneath—
sharp claws
sharp teeth.

Underneath the canopy,
things that sting and bite
and squeeze and crush.

Adrenaline rush.

And you at night;
the bugs come out
and feed well.

Give it a spell
and I will tell you—
I'd like for us to marry.

If only I could read your mind
before I open my mouth; please be kind.

I mean well!

Let Me Explain

Let me explain
once again:
the pain you will feel
will surely serve you right.

Last night,
like so many in the past,
I was aghast to find him in bed with you.

Our bed…

Our *marital* bed

He looked scared,
but you didn't care…
until the knife in my hand
came into play.
Then you both screamed the night away.

So let me explain
once again;
the pain you will feel
is your own fault, my angel.

I Need a Doctor

I want to see a doctor;
I want to see him today.
I have an illness
that just won't go away.

It's my heart, you see—
crushed and torn and bleeding.

The wife knows;
I catch her singing.
It is her, you see,
and those other men;
not just once
but again, and again.

My poor heart can't take it any more,
especially now you've walked out the door and out of my life.

Just Go

Why don't you go
the other way
and leave me alone?

I want you gone,
out of our house.
Go back to him,

Fall into his arms and cry,
saying how I did you wrong…
but we know the truth,
you and I.

Just go;
I don't want you any more.
Let him have you,
and believe me—
he's welcome to you.

And if I could, I'd shake his bloody hand!

Sleep? What's Sleep?

Sleep.
What's sleep?

I know it's something I need—
some place to rest,
to dream.

Dream of loved ones,
your pets,
work,
holidays.

Something to look forward to.
But the night frightens me;
the nights for me are ones of fear
and dread.

I know…
I know what awaits me.
Nightmares,
terrors

…and the longing for death.

A Fiery Embrace

And at the end of time,
man will be held to account
for what he's done.

And all of heaven
will sit in silence
and judge him.

And when the book of life is closed,
man will be cast away
into the fiery embrace of hell.

Unsightly

Iron bars
rusted with age,

cold stone walls
complete the cage;

heavy steel doors
locked at night

to keep all the convicts
out of sight.

Junkie

There's a junkie
lives down our street;
giant of a man
with cloven feet.

His hands are large
and hairy too;
he'll even sell drugs to you.

His teeth are long
and very sharp,
can't stand the sound of the lovely harp.

I don't know his name
or where to begin—
except he boasts of being the father of all sin.

Two Small Children

From out of madness
a new world was born.

The destruction
and desolation
of the war
destroyed all.

Nothing survived.
No plant,
no animal,
no fish…
all were gone.

Except…
two children;
such small children.
And their names
are hope and forgiveness.

Two Young Lovers

Two young lovers
slowly walk hand in hand,
leaving damp footprints behind
in soft warm sand.

The wind is gently blowing,
two hearts murmuring low;
bright stars laying in black velvet
set the heavens aglow.

Nervous eyes search his deeply,
looking for true love,
reflecting soft light from the stars
which are shining high above.

A trembling sigh disturbs the darkness
and rises slowly through the night;
strong arms gently enfold her
and embrace her so tight.

Loving words whispered softly;
two hearts now entwined.
And in each other's arms that night,
the world is left behind.

The wind is gently blowing,
two hearts murmur low;
tears of love slowly rising
and in the darkness, they begin to flow.

And as waves shyly roll in
and climb silently ashore,
two hearts now beat as one
and will forever more.

Tears That Burn

You've changed your mind?
Well, that's fine.
But let me say
I've been good to you
over the days.

And as they rolled
into years, I've never cried
so many tears.

Broken my heart,
broken my soul—
was this your goal?

Tell me now
before you go,
were you ever
my lover, or my foe?

I wish you would tell me so.

Here I am
on my own,
and you have gone back
to your old home

where your man has waited
all these years;
patiently waiting
for your return.

Now it's me who cries.

Will I ever learn?
Through tears that sting
and tears that burn.

Happy Tears

I look back
over the years
to when I first
met my wife.

We lived and loved
a lifetime together.

Hand in hand
we would walk;
sweet nothings
we would talk.

And on a Sunday
she would cook a roast;
I'd carve the meat
and give her most.

Look into her eyes
and she into mine,
looking deep
and we would find

love and contentment
over the years—
and looking at her, I cry happy tears.

Bindweed Around My Heart

There's no way
you're coming in;
I've lost enough skin
fighting over you.

Shout as much as you like,
I knew it was wrong to fall for you.

The local bike
is what you are called.

We were together just three years
and in that time I've cried many a tear.

Couldn't be faithful for that short time,
and the tears you now cry
are sweet and sour.

No longer are you
my beautiful flower;
now you're just bindweed around my heart…
and I loathe you for it!

Why Does the Wind Sigh?

Why does the wind sigh
for the tears of the willow tree?

Was it me who made her cry
when I carved our names high
and deep in her bark

that dark moonless night
when love shone bright
high in the heavens
all those years ago?

Does she still cry in pain
for a love so vain
and destined to fail?

Tesco

3:05 a.m.
Woke with the dregs
of another nightmare—
bad one this time.

Woke the wife scared;
she made me a cup of tea,
played a few hands of cards
just to bring me down.

Told her
I couldn't face shopping later that day,
not with all those people.
Without looking up from her cards
she said, "Why not do it now then?"

So here we are, 4.30 a.m.
and getting ready for Tesco,
it's like being a little boy all over again
when mum and dad were taking me down the coast for the day.

Exhilarating!

To Find a Woman

To find a woman
as beautiful as you,
a man could search his whole life through.

For in my eyes, darling,
you're worth more than gold
and I long to be near you
to love and to hold.

To taste your sweet kisses
once again,
and feel your caress
to ease this pain.

To love you gently
in the fading light,
and feel you sleeping softly
in my arms at night.

Catch Me, Gran

Hurry and catch me—
I'm falling, I am.
I'll hurt myself badly
if you don't catch me, Gran.

Quickly, quickly,
I'm sure to fall;
look at me wobble on top of this wall.

You'll have to be fast
if you're to save me at all—
if you're to save me, Gran,
from a terrible fall.

Feed Me Sweet Kisses

Feed me throughout the day
with your kisses so sweet;
let me taste sugar candy
as our two lips meet.

Then fill my cup with more kisses
that taste as sweet as wine,
so that each one I drink
it will always be mine.

And then send me to bed
with tender kisses,
soft, warm and light,
to keep away the cold
through these dark wintery nights.

But when morning comes around,
please start over again—
because I will be hungry, my darling
for your sweet kisses again.

Something Cosy

Give me something cosy
to cuddle up to,
like football or golf
or a hot bowl of stew.

A nice warm fire
and a cold can of beer
while it's snowing outside;
we'll be warm in here.

Give me a bed at night
that's cosy for two;
one side for me
the other for you.

Too Many Miles

Too many miles,
not enough smiles
and all the while
she sleeps around.

Pound for pound
he's a patient man
and loves her true;
what to do?

Let her be or tell her to go?

No…

Turn a blind eye,
try not to cry
as you listen to her lies.

Blue skies and sunshine
leave me cold,
just like you
when I try to hold.

Ice in my veins,
heart gone bad;
all this cheating
driving me mad.

And you, my darling—
aren't you glad
I haven't killed you yet?

The Winds of War

Wind's picking up;
I see it in the trees.
Was this morning
a gentle, playful breeze.

It seems in a hurry,
wherever it's going.

It doesn't care.

Trees uprooted,
houses torn down,
fences flying through the air.

And all the while
it races through,
doesn't give a damn
for me and you.

It'll knock us flat on our backs
and just steam-roll through.

Summer Days

Summer days
with skies of blue,
writing in sand, "I love you."

Hearts beating faster,
eyes aglow;
love never ending,
walking slow.

Kisses warm and tender,
hands entwine,
knowing this girl
will forever be mine.

She Will Never Be Mine

I heard the sound
of a lonely heart
splitting and tearing
itself apart.

I heard the birth
of a tear drop
and watched it grow,
then I heard it falling
into the abyss below.

I heard a door slamming
for the last time
and knew she would
never again be mine.

Arms Open Wide

Dance, dance
upon your grave;
have friends round—
we'll have a rave.

They don't know
you're buried deep;
they all think you're at home,
fast asleep.

Music blaring,
laughter high;
they don't know
how you died.

I laughed that much
I could have cried;
greet one and all
with arms open wide.

Take the Tears

Take the tears
from a babe in arms
and the tender tones
as a mother calms.

Take that pain
when her child cries
and a heart that's crushed
when that child dies.

Then take that sorrow
and the grief she cannot hide,
and just for a moment
set your own cares aside.

Feel her loss and her pain.

And pray to God
you will never have to
feel this woman's pain
ever again!

Tears on a Windowpane

The house stays respectfully silent
as alone you softly cry,
watching as each tear falls
like raindrops from the sky.

Aching to reach out and comfort you
and to embrace you gently in its walls;
the house bears witness to the names
of your children you despairingly call.

Feeling your body tremble
as you sit there all alone
and hearing your silent wishes
that your children could return home.

If only time could be turned backwards
and your children were small once again,
then your arms wouldn't feel so empty
and your heart be in so much pain.

But time moves swiftly forwards
and the seasons become as one,
and all you have are memories
of the things with your children you have done.

And all the while, the house has been watching,
saddened by your pain,
as a single tear drop falls silently
down the old, misted windowpane.

A Lonely Man

A man sits quietly
at the table in his cell
and listens to the distant chimes
of a lone church bell.

His heart grows heavy
each time the bell rings;
in his mind he sees the choir
and can hear the songs that they sing

with their voices raising gently
to our Lord in the sky,
oblivious to the tears
that this lone man cries.

Their voices and hearts
are filled with love
as they sing their praises
to the Lord above.

Singing their devotion,
how they will forgive and forget—
but not one of them has given a thought
to this lone man yet.

And so, with the last toll of the bell,
this man sits alone
with nothing but tears and thoughts
for his loved ones at home.

He will wait patiently for the day
when the bell rings again,
rekindling his heartache,
loneliness
and pain.

And then his tears will fall
free once more;
tears he has cried
so many times before.

Sad As Can Be

Birthday cards
that are pinned to the wall;
presents of toys
are given by all.

Jelly and ice-cream,
sweets and cakes;
these things, my darling,
your birthday will make.

Loud music and laughter
and games to play—
enjoy them, darling,
for this is *your* day.

There will be cuddles and kisses
from family and friends,
but my kisses will come
in the letters I send.

I wish things could be different
and I was set free,
because I miss you so very much
and I'm as sad as can be!

Daylight Is Fading

Daylight is fading
and the night draws near;
you've played out your games
and cried your last tear.

Your imaginary friends
have all gone away
and your eyes grow weary
through the games that you've played.

Books and crayons
have been put away,
and the pictures you've drawn
by your bedside will stay.

Your teddies and dollies
have all gone to sleep
and the secrets you've told them
they have promised to keep.

Your eyes feel so heavy
as mummy puts you to bed,
and soon the sandman will come
and dance softly inside your sweet head.

Then you will dream sweet dreams,
my darling,
all through the night,
as the sandman dances softly
until the early morning light.

Happy Fools

It's war! It's war!
The cry arose happily
throughout the land;
everyone clapped
and held hands.

Parties were held
out in the streets,
children danced around
in bare feet.

Women cried
with the good news;
men were flustered
at what units to choose.

Banners high,
banners low,
like the waves on the ocean
banners flowed.
Kisses goodbye;
kisses too late
for the young men
who marched cheerfully
to meet…
their deadly fate.

What I Had for Dinner

Guess what I had for dinner?

    Dead
animal flesh
    and

    murdered,
    butchered,
    skinned,
    boiled veg.

The leg of the
  chicken
we put in a
roasting pan.

  The veg
went the same way.

Everything boiled,
  bleeding,
   dying…

a bit like my wedding night.

Also Available

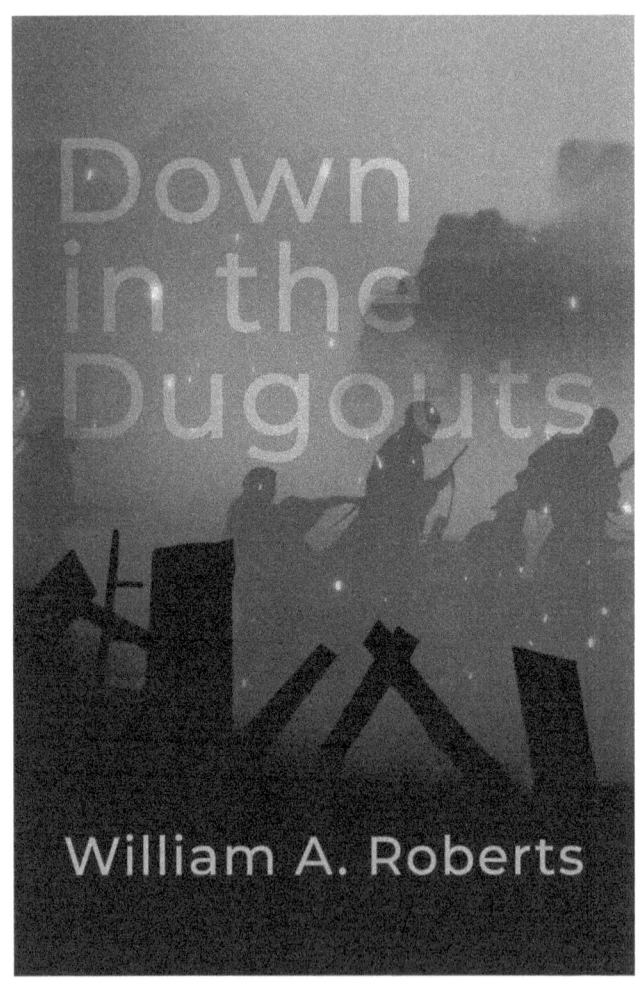

www.ingramcontent.com/pod-product-compliance
Lightning Source LLC
LaVergne TN
LVHW041624070426
835507LV00008B/437